Freeing the Voice

Mindfulness in Singing and Vocal Training

Table of Contents

Chapter 1. Introduction

Unleash the symphony within you! Our Special Report, "Freeing the Voice: Mindfulness in Singing and Vocal Training," dives into the intricate coalescence of mindfulness and vocal prowess, imbuing every note you vocalize with intention and authenticity. This captivating exploration is neither overly technical nor abstruse, making it an enjoyable read for both amateur vocalists and seasoned performers. Tune into your senses, harmonize with your voice, and embark on this enlightening journey of self-discovery. Indeed, the opportunity to uncover your true vocal potential awaits you within these pages. This special report might just be the key to not only finding your voice, but setting it free. So why wait? Sing your heart out, and let your voice resonate with the world!

Chapter 2. The Resonance of Mindfulness and Singing

Mindfulness encourages an in-the-moment awareness of our thoughts, feelings, and bodily sensations, an awareness that acts as the underpinning philosophy for many forms of meditation and therapy. In the context of singing, the role of mindfulness becomes imminently profound, transforming each note and pitch into an intentional expression of our inner landscape.

2.1. The Power of Being Present

We begin our exploration in the subtle art of being present. This act is the heart and soul of mindfulness, where one embodies the unfolding present moment fully. It will have a profound impact on your singing, transforming it into a more genuine and heartfelt expression. When our full presence is tuned to the task at hand, every note becomes a conscious decision, every word sung becomes a purposeful conveyance of feelings.

Being actively present aids in minimizing our wandering thoughts and mental chatter, which often prevents us from harnessing our full vocal potential. It allows us to accurately assess our vocal capabilities, voice control, and resonance, fostering an environment where we can genuinely connect with our audience.

2.2. Harnessing Inner Silence

Cultivating mindfulness within our singing practices entails harnessing silence, the scaffold upon which music and words find structure and meaning. Within the silence, the nuances of every phrase sung and every note hit can be better appreciated. Understanding the power of silence in song can amplify the impact of your voice, facilitating a more profound connection with your listeners.

By utilizing mindfulness, we learn in essence to sing from the quietude of our minds, enabling us to express with vocal resonance that mirrors the emotional depth of our inner silence. Harnessing these periods of silence not only improves our singing, but also enhances our understanding of the role silence plays in grounding us, in between and sometimes within a melody.

2.3. The Breath and Mindfulness

Breath—the life force that drives our voice and singing—is another significant aspect where mindfulness proves influential. Mastery in controlling and using the breath is crucial in achieving vocal prowess. When mindfulness accompanies the concept of breathing, the resulting vocal output can be transformational.

Mindfully attending to each inhalation and exhalation can help us monitor any unnecessary tension, and facilitate an understanding of how best to ration our breath over phrases and maintain vocal quality over the duration of the song. By consciously connecting with our breath, we not only enhance our vocal capacity, but also establish a sense of calm and peace within ourselves.

=⇒ Body Awareness and Vocal Technique

The inclusion of our corporeal dimension in this exploration is essential, as singing involves the entire body: from the diaphragm's distinct upward and downward movements, to the minute vibrations felt at the vocal folds, even down to the grounded stance of your feet. Such awareness facilitates subtle nuances of vocal control and modulation.

Body-awareness—one of the most enriching offshoots of mindfulness—coupled with regular vocal training, helps in refining vocal technique and enhancing live performance. This is valuable to both beginner vocalists who are grappling with the basics of posture, diaphragm control, and vocal articulation, and seasoned singers who aim for consistent performance quality, control over greater pitch range, and expressivity.

2.4. Emotional Transparency and Authenticity

Impressively, mindfulness also forges a deeper connection with our emotions, thereby ensuring an authentic emotive delivery in our singing. Having the capability to intentionally tap into the emotional reservoir of a song, and deliver it convincingly is an attribute of wonderful performers, often distinguishing them from good singers.

Understanding and working with our emotions is a gradual process sharpened by mindfulness, a tool to explore stages of joy, sorrow, excitement, and tranquility that music embodies. This emotional transparency allows your singing to resonate on a deeper level, transcending mere auditory enjoyment to a shared human experience.

2.5. The Noble Connection with the Audience

One of the most gratifying aspects of singing is the ability to forge a noble connection with listeners. Here, mindfulness serves as a bridge that allows for a beautifully shared moment of human expression. Singing with complete presence, emotion, and authenticity, your voice transforms into not just a conduit of music, but a medium of personal narrative and shared experiences.

In conclusion, the resonance of mindfulness and singing creates a powerful symphony, enabling a singer to be profoundly present, emotionally connected, technically refined, and genuinely resonating. Approaching singing with mindfulness is akin to treating it as a sacred act of expression, enriching the singing process as much as the receiving of it. The journey to freeing your voice begins with the awakened sense of self. The symphony awaits, not only to acquaint you with your voice, but unveil its unexplored potential. Embark on this journey of self-discovery, tune in with your senses, and resonate your voice with the world.

Chapter 3. Mindful Breathing: The Fundamental of Singing

Breathing: the essence of life and the bedrock foundation for mindful singing. It is where our journey starts, exploring the depths and nuances of this elementary yet significant practice. Indeed, breathing is more than just the act of inhaling and exhaling; it is the dynamic interplay of mindfulness, body, and sound.

3.1. The Anatomy of Breath

Understanding the physiology of breathing is instrumental to master the control of breath for singing. The breath emerges from the lungs, which serve as the primary storage of air in the body. The diaphragm, the primary muscle of respiration, lies beneath the lungs. In essence, as we inhale, the diaphragm contracts, moving downwards and causing the lungs to expand. This expansion creates a vacuum that draws air in. As we exhale, the diaphragm relaxes, returning upwards, and the lungs shrivel, expelling air.

Thanks to this dynamic process, breath becomes a vehicle for our voice. The expelled air during exhalation navigates through the voice box, or larynx, vibrating the vocal folds and generating sound. This sound then traverses the vocal tract, which works as the resonating chamber to amplify and modify the tone.

3.2. Mindful Breathing: The Lifeline of Singing

Once this physiological groundwork is laid, we can delve into the crux of this chapter: mindful breathing. Mindfulness, in essence, involves being present and fully engaged, aware of our feelings, thoughts, and bodily sensations without judgment. It provides singers with a powerful toolset for mastery, fostering increased control, relaxation, and expressivity.

To breathe mindfully, one needs to engage in conscious breath control. This process involves two integral components: inhalation and exhalation, both of which require an acute awareness of the body and sensory perceptions. On inhaling, sense the shape, rhythm, and weight of your own breath. What do you feel as the air passes through your nostrils, filling your lungs and expanding your diaphragm? Upon exhaling, can you feel the release, the lightness creeping over your body? Breathe in peace and harmony, exhale stress and anxiety.

3.3. Breathing Exercise: Five-Senses Exploration

Let's now immerse ourselves in a simple, holistic exercise that leverages your five senses—smell, touch, taste, sight, and hearing—to aid in mindful breathing.

1. **Smell:** As you inhale, bring your attention to the smells around you. Visualize the breath enveloping all these ambient scents, carrying them inward into your lungs.

2. **Touch:** As you hold the breath, feel the subtle rise and fall of your abdomen. Feel the air filling your lungs, expanding your diaphragm.

3. **Taste:** As you slowly release the breath, notice the taste of it leaving your mouth.

4. **Sight:** Keep your eyes closed during this exercise. As you breathe, visualize the airflow as waves of energy.

5. **Hearing:** Listen to the sound of your breathing, unfiltered and unadjudicated. The gentle rustle akin to wind — or the ocean's ebb — is your rhythm, your symphony.

Repeat this exercise until the awareness and control of breath become second nature. Return to it whenever you need grounding or find your thoughts to be jumbled during a performance.

3.4. Expanding Your Breath Capacity

Expanding breath capacity is particularly essential for singers as it facilitates sustainment of longer phrases and notes. Here, the key lies in effectively deploying the diaphragm and engaging in diaphragmatic or "deep" breathing. This breathing technique will not only improve breath control but also promote relaxation and relief from physical and mental tension.

Let's exercise: Take a slow, deep breath, filling the belly, ribcage, and back with air. Pay attention to your diaphragm, feeling it lower as your lungs expand. Exhale slowly, sense the diaphragm rise back to its original position. Make sure you do this without forcing the breath or straining.

3.5. The Marriage between Breath and Voice

Having established a foundation of mindful breathing and breath control, we now turn our focus toward combining breath and voice.

Delve into your breath as you produce a sung tone. Can you feel the same sense of presence, awareness, and peace as before? Remember, your voice is an extension of your breath—you do not "create" it, you "allow" it to exist and resonate. When you sing, humble your heart to the uniqueness of your voice, and let your breath tell your story, with the lyrics and melody delivering the essence of your emotions.

3.6. Concluding Remarks

As we conclude this chapter, we hope your understanding of the role that mindful breathing plays in singing has deepened. Just as breathing gives life, it too gives life to your singing, rooting it in intention and authenticity.

Remember, the journey to mastering mindfulness in singing is ongoing. It is not about perfection but about growth and understanding. Embrace the transformations, the ebbs & flows, and ultimately find harmony between your breath, voice, and mindfulness. This sonic symbiosis will enable you to explore your vocal potential, illuminating your path to unearthing and liberating your authentic voice.

Chapter 4. Understanding your Vocal Identity

Just as a painter understands his palette, a singer must recognize the distinct qualities of their voice to make the most remarkable masterpiece. In our journey, the first step is coming to terms with the notion of our voice as an instrument and recognizing its unique identity.

4.1. The Conceptual Framework of Vocal Identity

The concept of vocal identity centers around the unique qualities and dimensions of your voice. It's both an auditory and psychological construct, defining not just how you sound physically but also how you connect emotionally and mentally with your vocals.

Famed operatic conductor Colin Davis once said, "The voice is an instrument that contains emotion". Herein lies the inherent richness of the voice; it is at once a musical instrument and a medium for conveying emotions. It's deeply personal and, often, an intrinsic part of our identity.

To understand your vocal identity, think of elements like timbre, range, vocal weight or type, registers, flexibility, tessitura, vocal resonances, and more. Reflect upon your natural pronunciation, your habitual rhythms, and how you naturally stress syllables. All these components interplay until they converge into your unique voice or vocal signature.

4.2. Unraveling the Physical Aspects

Embarking on the journey to discover your vocal identity, you must first unravel the physical aspects of your voice. Delving into the wide-ranging aspects of your vocal instrument might seem daunting, but it's a rewarding task.

The first physical dimension of your voice to assess is vocal range. It is the spectrum of pitches that you can comfortably and consistently sing, from the lowest note to the highest. Many vocal pedagogues encourage their students to focus on their 'comfortable range' initially, before progressively expanding it.

Once you've identified your range, move to vocal weight or vocal type. This is the characteristic sound of your voice that defines its color and personality. Are you a light and bright Soprano or a full and strong Bass?

Next, explore your vocal registers. A vocal register is a series of consecutive notes that share a similar timbre and vibratory pattern. Singing comfortably in different registers like chest voice, head voice, and falsetto can reflect different parts of your vocal identity.

Understanding your tessitura, or the range in which your voice is most comfortable and effective, is another integral part of defining your voice. It doesn't necessarily align with the absolute highest or lowest notes you can hit, but rather where your voice 'sits' comfortably.

Lastly, understand the resonant characteristics of your voice. This is defined by how your body influences the sound of your voice, creating unique sonic textures and colors.

4.3. Emotional Resonance: Making Your Voice Heard

Having grasped the physical aspects, let's turn towards the emotional resonance. Mastering this aspect allows you to perform not just with your voice but 'through' it.

Emotional resonance means connecting with your vocal emissions, magnifying your performance with heartfelt authenticity. Achieving emotional resonance begins with introspection. Grasp the emotion tied to a piece of music or lyric and embrace that feeling.

Strive for interpretative empathy, letting the words flow naturally with clear articulation. Command the nuances of dynamics, phrasing, and rhythm, all of which can deepen the emotional resonance.

Also, understand that every vocal mistake is a learning opportunity. Embrace them as they reveal the areas that need the most work. Your journey is your own, inherently personal, and unique. Cherish every step you take towards understanding your vocal identity.

4.4. Engaging the Mind-Body Connection

With physical and emotional elements in place, understanding the mind-body connection in singing can take your vocal identity to the next level. Singing is not just physical or emotional; it's a holistic engagement of both. How you hold yourself while singing, your breath control, facial expression, and even your mental state can influence your voice.

Practice mindfulness and body awareness to better understand the sensations of singing. Notice how your body feels as you breathe in and out, how your abdomen rises and falls, how each note resonates within you. This synesthetic approach can crystalize your connection to your voice, deepening your understanding of your vocal identity.

In conclusion, understanding one's vocal identity is truly a voyage of self-discovery. Your vocal instrument is uniquely yours, an auditory and emotional fingerprint that can leave a lasting sonic impact. Being mindful of your voice's physical attributes while also nourishing emotional engagement and a mind-body connection can enhance your personal vocal quality. This, in essence, is the harmonious symphony within you, a melody composed of authenticity, consciousness, and self-expression, waiting to resonate with the world.

Chapter 5. The Power of Intention in Vocal Expression

To begin our exploration of vocal expression, we start by delving into the role and importance of intention. Intention is the driving force underpinning every successful endeavor in life, providing the energy necessary to propel any action. The same applies to singing where every note carries a weight of meaning, a palette of colors, and an undercurrent of emotion - all scaffolded by the power of intention.

5.1. The Concept of Intention in Vocal Expression

In the realm of vocal expression, 'intention' refers to the deliberate act of vocalizing articulated sounds charged with specific emotions, connotations, and thoughts. This involves both the conscious and subconscious mind to create and convey a precise musical and emotional message.

An exploration of intention is not confined solely to the realm of music; it's a integral element deeply embedded in human communication. The significance of intention is seen in the way we speak, in our body language, and in our emotive expressions. Therapists and communication experts employ myriad techniques that revolve around the idea of intention to enable better interpersonal understanding and facilitate healing.

When translating this concept into the realm of singing, we extend the communication not just through language, but through musical sound - a language universally understood, unbound by cultural limitations and geographic boundaries.

So, the next question then becomes, how do we channel this concept of intention into our vocal expression?

5.2. Techniques to Integrate Intention in Singing

The integration of intention in your vocal practice is more of an internal journey rather than an external one. It is about creating a conscious connection between your mind, body, and voice. Following are some techniques that can guide you on this journey:

1. Mindful Breathing: Mindful breathing is an effective way to form the bridge between the conscious and the subconscious. In this practice, one needs to focus on the natural rhythm of the breath while singing. This anchors your consciousness in the present moment, allowing better control of your vocal output.

2. Emotional Resonance: Emotion fuels intention. By allowing yourself to fully feel and understand the emotions attached to the song, you'll infuse each note with authenticity, elevating your performance from simple sound production to a heartfelt expression.

3. Clear Articulation: The way you articulate words and phrases is crucial to conveying your intended message, making clarity and precision extremely important.

4. Visualization: There's considerable power in picturing the sound and delivery you aim to produce. Visualization techniques could consist of imagining the trajectory of your notes or envisioning the sonic color you wish your sound to possess.

Attempting to integrate these practices into your vocal rehearsals might initially feel daunting. However, with time and consistent practice, they'll become an inseparable part of your routine, enhancing the quality and ease of your performance.

5.3. The Role of Intention in Vocal Training

Just as in performance, the concept of intention is also invaluable in vocal training. Training with intention means focusing not just on the technical aspects, such as pitch or timbre, but also on understanding and harnessing the power of emotion, narrative, and individual identity within the music.

Vocal coaches often stress the importance of bringing your whole self to the performance, not just your vocal mechanics. Integral to this is being able to express your own stories, emotions, and life experiences through your voice. This, in essence, is what it means to sing with intention - connecting to the songs you sing on a personal level and reshaping them with your own personal narrative.

When training with intention, the repertoire selected for practice must align with your personal and emotional connection, as this facilitates a more genuine message and enhances interpretive skills. Moreover, these songs will resonate more intensely with your audience, creating a deeper impact.

Long-term, implementing intention in your vocal training and practice instills a sense of purpose and accountability, rendering you not just a singer, but a storyteller - a communicator of music and emotion.

5.4. Intention- A Bridge to Authentic Voice

The ultimate destination of your vocal journey should not only be about perfecting technique but also about finding your authentic voice. Intention is an integral part of this journey, acting as a bridge that connects your unique personal narrative, emotion, and experiences to your vocal expression.

Singing with intention lends credibility to your voice that resonates with the human condition, echoing raw emotions in their truest form. A voice rich with intention stands out not for its perfect technique, but for its ability to connect, penetrate, and move hearts, inciting visceral responses that transcend the artist-listener dynamic, fostering a shared human experience.

With intention shaping the contours of your vocals, your performance evolves into more than just an act of vocalization. It transforms into a journey, a revelation - an echo of shared life and experiences, leaving indelible traces in the sands of human emotion.

The journey to tracing your true vocal potential might be arduous, laced with self-doubt and teetering confidence. However, understanding, embracing and harnessing the power of intention will be a guiding light, navigating you towards the shores of successful, genuine, and impactful vocal expression.

So, set your sail, prepare your voice, and embark on an exhilarating voyage towards empowering your voice with intention. Remember, the power you seek to color your vocals with authenticity and to connect with your audience resides within you. Harness it, nurture it, and let the melody of your true voice flow unabated!

Chapter 6. Physical Relaxation: Finding Ease within Vocal Strain

Understanding the intricate relationship between your body and your voice is the first step towards achieving vocal ease and eliminating strain. Your voice is inherently intertwined with the physical condition. It depends greatly on the functioning of your musculature, your respiratory system, and various other interconnected systems that constitute your body.

6.1. The Role of Physical Relaxation

Muscles play a crucial role in the functioning of our vocal system. The diaphragm, a muscle located below the lungs, plays a vital role in controlling our breath, which in turn impacts our voice. Similarly, the muscles in the larynx, the organ encompassing the vocal cords, are critical in producing sound. The muscles of the throat and jaw also contribute significantly to vocal production.

Physical tension can directly impede these muscles from functioning optimally and fluidly. Tension in the jaw can restrict the open space needed for sound to resonate, while tension in the larynx can render us unable to hit certain pitches.

Relaxation techniques involve consciously releasing this muscle tension to restore your body to a more comfortable, neutral state. Achieving a relaxed, neutral state throughout your body can liberate your voice and allow it to achieve more depth, richness, and flexibility.

6.2. Body Awareness: A Precondition for Relaxation

Before you can begin to release physical tension, you must first become aware of it. This can be challenging since many of us carry tension unknowingly. Awareness can be cultivated through mindfulness, deliberate focus, and introspection.

Start by performing a body scan. This technique involves mentally scanning your body, from top to bottom, taking note of any sensations or tension. You can do this while sitting or lying down, whatever you find most comfortable. Breathe deeply and take your time with this process.

6.3. Breath Control: The Foundation of Vocal Relaxation

Awareness alone, however, is not enough. Once you've identified areas of tension, the next step is to actively work on releasing it through targeted relaxation exercises. One such technique is diaphragmatic breathing or abdominal breathing.

This technique involves deliberately engaging your diaphragm to take deeper, more controlled breaths. Start by lying down on your back. Place one hand on your chest and the other on your abdomen. Inhale deeply through your nose, filling your lungs from the bottom up. You should feel your abdomen rise and your chest remain relatively still. Exhale through your mouth, letting your abdomen fall naturally.

Practicing diaphragmatic breathing frequently can significantly boost your breath control, reduce tension, and enhance the richness and range of your voice.

6.4. Progressive Muscle Relaxation: A Systematic Approach

A more comprehensive approach to achieving physical relaxation is through Progressive Muscle Relaxation (PMR). Derived from the principles of psychology, PMR involves systematically tensing and then relaxing each muscle group sequentially.

Start with the muscles at the top of your head and gradually move down through your body, all the way to your toes. Pay attention to the contrasting sensations of tension and relaxation, and with each release of tension, imagine your voice flowing more freely.

PMR can help reduce the overall muscle tension in your body and improve your receptiveness to vocal training.

6.5. Vocal Warm-ups and Cool-downs

Just like any other physical exercise, exercising your voice also requires proper warm-ups and cool-downs. Warming up the vocal cords before singing or performing can prevent undue strain and improve performance.

Vocal warm-ups can include humming, lip trills, and scales, all done gently and at a comfortable pitch. After singing or performing, it's equally important to do vocal cool-downs. These could involve slow glides from high to low pitches and soft, sustained hums. They help to release any tension that may have been built up during your performance.

6.6. Strategic Hydration and Nutrition

Hydration and a balanced diet can also play a significant role in vocal health. The vocal cords vibrate very quickly and can become irritated and dry without proper hydration. Drinking plenty of water throughout the day, especially before and after singing, can help maintain vocal health.

Nutritionally, avoiding spicy foods and excessive caffeine can ward off irritation to your vocal cords. For some, dairy products may also cause mucus buildup, so they should be consumed strategically.

6.7. Relaxation Visualization Techniques

Visualization is a powerful tool for deepening relaxation and reducing performance anxiety. Imagine a space where you feel completely at ease. Visualize your song or piece coming effortlessly without strain or concern. Allow this peaceful image to infiltrate your mind, enhancing positivity and relaxation.

Combine this visualization with deep, conscious breathing exercises for enhanced benefit. These techniques in tandem can foster a relaxed state of body and mind, offering fertile ground for your voice to grow and thrive.

6.8. The Road to Mindful Vocal Training

Physical relaxation is not just about muscle release; it's also about cultivating a state of mind that supports your vocal journey. Through mindfulness, breath control, tension-reducing exercises, and vital lifestyle elements like hydration and nutrition, you can build a strong foundation for your vocal practice. By understanding your body and its interplay with your voice, you can find ease from vocal strain and unlock a more vibrant, resonant voice.

Chapter 7. Exploring the Emotional Spectrum of your Voice

Music, as legendary composer Robert Schumann once expressed, is "the perfect type of art." It's an expression of the wide-ranging and ever-changing emotional state of being human, providing listeners with an experiential peak into a vast spectrum of emotions – from joy to despair, from love to heartbreak and beyond. Even more fascinating, perhaps, is the realization that the same piece of music can evoke different emotions in different listeners, a phenomenon we've likely all experienced. But what about singers? How do singers negotiate this emotional landscape, and how can they harness the power of emotion to enhance their performance?

7.1. The Imperatives of Emotional Resonance

Understanding emotion in singing starts with understanding the concept of resonance. Resonance is more than just a technical term referring to the amplification and enrichment of tones. In a broader and more profound sense, resonance refers to the empathetic connections that music induces between the singer and the listener. It's these connections that make the music "come alive," transforming a simple melody into an emotive and captivating experience.

For singers, this means that the more resonant their performance, the more emotionally charged and thus impactful it becomes. To accomplish this, singers need to navigate their own emotional landscape, learning how to tap into, express, and control their emotions. Far from merely reciting lyrics over a melody, singers must resonate emotionally with their audience, making them feel each word and note.

7.2. Empathy: The Bridge between the Singer and the Audience

Empathy, or the ability to understand and share the feelings of others, plays a crucial role in emotionally engaging singing. When a singer employs empathy, they essentially step into another person's shoes and feel their emotions. Singers can conjure emotions within themselves, which are in tune with the emotions that the song expresses, and convey these emotions with their voice. The ability to do this effectively forms the essence of emotionally powerful and resonant performance.

Empathy can be engendered in several ways: by relating to the character of a song, by connecting with personal experiences that resonate with a song's narrative, or by creating an imaginary backdrop that invokes the desired emotions. The process of empathic engagement adds a layer of authenticity and emotional richness to a performance that listeners can sense and consequently reciprocate.

7.3. Techniques for Emotional Expression in Singing

Harnessing emotional expression is a skill that can be cultivated with practice and mindfulness. Here we offer several strategies to help singers engage more deeply with their emotions.

1. Connecting with the Lyrics: Almost every song tells a story, and these stories are typically infused with emotion. As singers, you should dive into the song's story, thinking about the emotions that underlie the lyrics. Connecting with the lyrics allows you to align your emotional state with the character or narrator of the song, facilitating a more authentic and emotive performance.

2. Visualizing Emotion: This technique involves a mindful visualization exercise where you associate each song or individual sections of a song with specific emotional states or scenarios. These visualizations can guide your emotional expression as you work through the song.

3. Singing with Emotional Intention: Every note sung should carry emotional intention. When singing a particular note or phrase, be aware of the emotion you want to convey, and use this intention to guide your vocal expressivity. Concentration and mindfulness come into play here, and the result can be deeply emotionally charged performances.

4. Musical Nuance: The use of dynamics, tone, rhythm, and phrasing can also be useful tools for singers seeking to enhance their emotional expressivity. Each of these musical elements can be manipulated to reflect and enhance the emotional theme of the song.

7.4. Emotional Authenticity: The Hallmark of Effective Emotional Expression

While it is possible to mimic or "perform" emotions, authenticity is key when dealing with emotional expression in singing. Authenticity refers to the truthful and honest portrayal of emotion, and it sets the stage for a genuinely engaging performance. No amount of technical skill can substitute for the truthful communication of emotional content, for this is what resonates with audiences and allows singers to connect at a deeply human level.

Using the techniques above, singers can start to discover their emotional palette and how best to use it in their singing. This emotional literacy, combined with a commitment to authenticity, enables singers to deliver deeply resonant and engaging performances that move their audience.

7.5. Negotiating the Emotional Landscape: Handling Difficult Emotions

While displaying emotion can enhance a performance, singers must also navigate particularly challenging emotional landscapes, such as extreme sadness, despair, or anger. These emotions are notoriously difficult to manage, and singers typically run the risk of becoming emotionally overwhelmed. Grasping how to express these emotions without being consumed by them is an essential skill. Mindfulness and self-awareness exercises can help with emotional regulation and control during performances.

As we have explored, emotions play an indispensable role in singing. They provide a medium through which singers can more deeply connect with their audiences and deliver resonant performances. Whether it's through empathetic engagement or the deliberate crafting of emotion through different techniques, singers stand to benefit from venturing into the emotional spectrum of their voice. After all, as nineteenth-century poet Henry Wadsworth Longfellow once declared, "Music is the universal language of mankind." And what is language but the extension of our emotional selves? So, fellow singers, venture forth bravely into this vast emotional landscape, and let your song resonate with all the depth and breadth of human experience.

Chapter 8. Building Strong Vocal Habits with Mindfulness

In the journey of aligning one's mind, body, and voice, the first step introduces us to the realm of establishing robust vocal habits bolstered by mindfulness. Mindfulness, in the context of singing, is far more than a passing fad or fashionable buzzword. It's a powerful, globally recognized method for reducing anxiety, sharpening focus, and improving overall well-being, elements crucial to enhancing vocal performance.

8.1. Understanding Mindfulness

At its core, mindfulness invites us to exist in the present moment without judgment. It's about being self-aware consciously, aware of our thoughts, feelings, senses, and surrounding environment. In singing, mindfulness helps vocalists connect more deeply on an emotional level with their voice, immersing themselves entirely in the act of singing or practicing.

8.2. The Mind-Voice Connection

Engaging the mind while singing involves focused attention and heightened awareness, both of which play decisive roles in performance. Our thoughts and emotions greatly influence our voice and its delivery — a happy mood may cause the voice to sound lively and energetic; conversely, when feeling low, the voice can be dull or shaky. Thus, understanding and managing the link between the mind and voice is vital for creating a vocal presentation that rings pure and true.

8.3. Embracing the Practice: Mindful Singing

Mindful singing refers to the practice of combining mindfulness and singing, an approach that offers a host of benefits. Mindful singers pay undivided attention to their vocal production — the physical sensations, movements, and emotions involved. This amplified focus enhances the connection with your voice, leading to better control and overall vocal performance.

8.4. Creating a Mindful Warm-up Routine

A crucial stepping stone in building strong vocal habits is setting up a mindful warm-up routine. Progressing from simple deep breathing and stretches, you then transition into vocal exercises like lip trills, sirens, or scales. Attention must be on the present moment throughout, focusing on the sensations of relaxation, stretching, and voice generation.

8.5. Exercises for Enhanced Breath Control

Taking the mindfulness-based approach to a notch, a series of exercises have proven extremely helpful. These exercises like 'Triangle Breathing', 'Extended Exhale', and the 'Paced Breath Sequence,' concentrated on paced and mindful breathing, are crucial in enhancing breath control. This control is central for a singer, and being more mindful of breath supports modulation and sustained singing sequences.

8.6. Recognizing and Releasing Tension

Over time, tension builds up in the body, impairing control of our voice. To address this, deliberate, mindful body scanning can help identify areas of tension. Deep muscular relaxation exercises then allow for the release of this accumulated tension, bringing relief and restoring the fluidity and tone of your voice.

8.7. Mindfulness in Practice: Singing Meditation

Another way to incorporate mindfulness into your vocal habits is through singing meditation. In this process, you effortlessly let the melody flow without worrying about perfection. The focus is not on hitting the right notes but the act of singing itself. This process brings about profound relaxation, enhancing vocal capacity in unexpected ways.

8.8. The Balancing Act: Vocal Rest and Vocal Hygiene

Finally, an often-underestimated element in building strong vocal habits is the practice of vocal rest and hygiene. Maintaining a routine that includes enough sleep, proper hydration, a balanced diet, and avoiding harmful vocal practices strengthens our voice's resilience and longevity.

8.9. Reflection and Continuity: The Role of Journaling

Journaling your singing practice can be a highly effective tool in your mindfulness journey. By documenting your practices, patterns, challenges, triumphs, and feelings before and after each singing session, you gain a greater understanding and awareness of your progress. This documentation encourages continuity and self-observation, instrumental for ongoing improvement.

In conclusion, marrying mindfulness and singing is like creating a beautifully intricate tapestry where each thread contributes to the overall picture. When woven together, these threads form a strong fabric of sound, emotion, and expression. Becoming a mindful singer starts by building strong vocal habits, focusing on every aspect from warming up, exercising, recognizing and releasing tension, to mindful meditation and vocal care. As you take this journey, let mindfulness guide and fill every corner of your vocal life.

Chapter 9. Sharpening Awareness: The Key to Vocal Mastery

Before we delve into the mechanics and methodology of vocal training, it is crucial to understand the concept of 'awareness.' Awareness, in essence, is a state of being acutely engaged and mindful of our entire being - physical, emotional, and spiritual. In the context of singing, awareness is the cornerstone of vocal mastery as it brings focus to breath control, pitch precision, vocal resonance, diction, and emotional embodiment.

9.1. Breath Control: The Foundation of Vocal Technique

Breath control is the basic pillar of any vocal technique. Often neglected or taken for granted, proper breath management can be the difference between a good performance and a great one. It isn't just about taking in enough air; it is primarily about how you use it to support your voice while you sing.

Begin by laying on the floor, placing your hands onto your belly. As you inhale, feel your diaphragm pushing outward, forcing your hands to rise. As you exhale, your hands will naturally lower. This simple exercise helps to enhance your awareness of your breath. Please repeat this exercise daily, until you can be conscious of the subtle expansion and contraction of your diaphragm while standing and singing.

9.2. Pitch Precision: Accuracy Meets Emotion

Accuracy in pitching is an attribute of good singers. Whether using relative pitch or perfect pitch, a singer needs to have an incredible "inner ear" to discern the different notes. This is best achieved through active listening, not just passive.

One way to enhance this skill is by repeatedly listening to a piece of music and attempting to duplicate the notes. Start with simple songs, gradually working your way up to more complex pieces.

However, as important as technical precision is, music isn't merely clinical accuracy. It's about evoking and interpreting emotions. So, thoughtfully leverage the pitches: use lower pitches to convey calm and peace, while employing higher pitches to express excitement or urgency. Remember, accuracy without emotion makes for mundane music.

9.3. Vocal Resonance: Fine-tuning our Natural Amps

Every voice is unique and contains a richness that, when discovered, can contribute to a beautiful, resonant sound. Resonance is achieved when the sounds produced in our vocal cords are amplified and enriched within various cavities in our head.

To explore your resonance, try humming. Notice how the sound feels as it vibrates in your throat, mouth, and nose. Experiment with different pitches and notice changes. This ongoing experiment can help cultivate the sense of applying proper resonance in different ranges, allowing for a fuller, more resonant voice.

9.4. Diction and Articulation: Clarity in Expression

Clear diction is vital in singing. It's not just about having a beautiful voice; it's ensuring your listeners can understand what you're singing. Incorporate tongue twisters into your warm-up sessions, improving both agility and accuracy of speech.

When it comes to languages, immerse yourself in the phonetics and rhythms of different languages. This allows for more authentic renditions of songs in non-native languages.

9.5. Emotion Embodiment: The Core of Singing

Singing isn't just about getting the mechanics right; it's about communicating a story, a feeling, an experience. The ability to incorporate the right emotion(s) into your vocal delivery is an important piece of the singing puzzle. This requires you to harness all the other elements - breath control, pitch precision, vocal resonance and diction - with an emotional undercurrent.

Take time to understand the lyrics, research their context, and identify the emotions. This will help shape your interpretation and delivery.

In conclusion, becoming acutely aware of the interconnected elements of singing is the key to mastering your voice. Over time, these practices become second-nature. Moment-to-moment awareness molds a singer in their methods, style, and performance. This mindful approach to singing paves the way for an expressive, compelling, and resonant voice.

Chapter 10. Enriching Performance with Mindful Singing

Singing, truly, is a celebration of the human spirit, and to harness its true potential, an understanding of the role mindfulness plays in the equation is essential.

In the quest to enrich one's performance, it all begins with awareness, the fundamental cornerstone of mindful singing. This journey of self-discovery and genuine vocal expression calls for deep introspection and heightened attention to both our internal and external world.

10.1. Understanding Mindfulness

Mindfulness, rooted in the millennia-old tradition of Buddhist meditation, is an aspect of human consciousness associated with attention, awareness, and presence. Mindfulness allows us to attune to the rich tapestry of sensations, feelings, thoughts, and external events without judgment or avoidance.

A mindful approach to singing involves precisely this kind of awareness, where every iota of sound, every minute physical sensation, and the living relationship between breath, body, and voice become the focus of intense observation. By immersing ourselves in the 'here and now', we open up an untrodden path towards authenticity and expression that enriches our performance.

10.2. Integrating Mindfulness in Singing

Incorporating mindfulness into singing requires a multi-pronged approach focusing on cultivating presence, bodily sensations, and understanding emotions. Each aspect forms a critical component of vocal performance, illuminating the interplay between the physical, emotional, and cerebral elements of singing.

10.2.1. Presence

Presence is about being in the moment, feeling every note, and expressing it with intention. When you sing, ensure your entire being is within that musical note you are producing. Instead of thinking of the next line or how the audience is perceiving you, invest your full attention in the present. Use each inhalation and exhalation to connect deeper with your sound, without anticipating the next breath or note.

10.2.2. Sensing Transparency

Mindfulness in singing calls for complete transparency with our body and its sensations. As you sing, pay heed to the vibrations that each note stimulates, how your diaphragm expands and contracts, how your jaw opens, and how your palate shifts. This intimate awareness of your body will align your physicality with your vocal delivery, enriching the performance.

10.2.3. Emotional Understanding

Plumbing the depths of our emotions is a cornerstone of mindfulness. We need to acknowledge and embrace our emotions, as they give life to the lyrics we sing. Instead of succumbing to stage fright or suppressing nervousness, recognize these feelings, examine them without judgement, and channel them into your performance. By accepting and understanding our emotions, we imbue our words with true, unfiltered feeling.

10.3. The Breathing Bridge

Breath is the backbone of both singing and mindfulness. The breath forms a bridge between our body and mind, creating a feedback loop of awareness between our physical sensations and mental state. By focusing on the rhythm, depth and flow of breath, we can learn to control the voice, manage our performance anxieties, and ultimately enhance our performance.

10.3.1. Breath Awareness

Begin singing with a deep breath, feeling it fill your lungs and spread through your body. Become aware of how this breath fuels your sound. When mindfulness and singing converge on the crossroad of breath, it fosters an intimate connection between the internal state of mind and the expressive singing voice.

10.3.2. Breath Control

Controlling our breath is crucial for tone modulation and sustained singing. The art of modulating our breath can be honed through mindfulness, where we bring our consciousness to every inhalation and exhalation, and gradually learn to modulate it, enhancing our control over our notes and phrases.

10.4. The Resonance of Mindfulness

Ultimately, the union of singing and mindfulness culminates in a resonant performance that is indicative of the singer's true self. This resonance stems from a state of heightened awareness and authenticity, turning a mere vocal performance into an expressive, captivating, and real display of human emotion.

Singing is not just about the voice; it's an amalgamation of mind and body, thoughts, emotions, and physical sensations. By applying mindfulness techniques to singing, we are not only fostering a more powerful and controlled voice, but also facilitating a dynamic and emotionally resonant performance. By peeling away the layers of pretense, we uncover the authentic voice within us, providing an enhanced, genuine connection with the audience that can be both fulfilling and transformative.

The journey to enriching performance in singing is a quest for authenticity, a thirst for realness. By integrating mindfulness into our practice, we allow ourselves to explore the depths of our voice and overall performance. Mindfulness engenders a non-judgmental self-awareness that sets the stage for expressing the pure, unadulterated human spirit. When we truly realize this state of being, we allow ourselves to be free and fully express the voice within.

Chapter 11. Journey of Continuous Improvement: Mindfulness in Practice

In a world where constant activity and hustle are often valorized, adopting mindfulness might seem contrary, but its application to singing and voice improvement can't be underestimated. When embedded in practice, mindfulness becomes a beacon guiding you on the ever-evolving journey of continuous improvement.

11.1. Attention and Awareness

Every spectacular performance relies on two crucial elements: attention and awareness. Many people interchange these terms, but in the realm of mindfulness, they hold unique positions. Attention corresponds to the ability to focus on a specific task or sound, in this case, your voice. On the other hand, awareness encapsulates a broader scope, the ability to apprehend every nuance of our experience without judgment.

For singers, developing these two capacities has tangible benefits. Cultivating attention enables one to concentrate on the minutiae of their voice—pitch, tone, breath control—while awareness allows capturing the totality of the experience—the emotions, feelings, and broader context of the performance.

11.2. The Mindfulness Paradox

Practicing mindfulness might initially seem like a paradox; staying tranquil while singing or vocalizing can be challenging. However, mindfulness isn't about suppressing activity or forcing calmness. Instead, it involves witnessing your vocal practices as they are, intentionally and without judgment.

Acknowledge the paradox within mindfulness and singing, then step into the space it creates. Allow yourself to feel the rhythm, be engrossed in the harmonies, absorb the power of lyrics, and express these elements through your vocals without self-critique or anxiety. It's a process of becoming present with the music, your voice, and the emotions they stir.

11.3. Breath: The Bridge to Mindfulness

Breath is the bridge connecting the body and mind, a crucial element in both singing and mindfulness. Singers understand the importance of breath control, yet mindfulness adds an extra layer of understanding to this process. Being consciously aware of your breath as you sing can bring you into the present moment, anchoring you into a state of mindfulness.

Exercises involving deep inhales and controlled exhales can be the first step to incorporating mindfulness to your singing. This connection between breath and singing prepares not just your body, but also your mind, for the journey ahead.

11.4. Body Scan: A Tool for Singers

As a segue to applied mindfulness, body scanning can be an instrumental process. It involves going through each part of your body mentally, acknowledging tensions, stiffness or relaxation. Singing involves whole-body participation, making this technique particularly useful to detect and relieve tension areas that might affect your vocal production.

Start with your toes, gradually moving up, and pay attention to the way your body feels. As you extend your awareness to the parts engaged in singing—abdominal muscles, chest, throat, mouth, and facial muscles—you'll find yourself more in tune with your physicality, which directly influences how you express your voice.

11.5. Emotional Resonance

Emotional resonance in singing isn't solely about conveying the emotion intrinsic in the song. It also involves resonating with personal feelings and emotions during the performance. Mindfulness can assist in achieving a deeper emotional resonance by bringing into awareness unaddressed or suppressed feelings, thereby enriching your vocal representation.

The beauty of singing lies not just in hitting the right notes but in pouring your heart and soul into each performance. As the legendary singer Billie Holiday beautifully expressed, "If I'm going to sing like someone else, then I don't need to sing at all." Singing with authenticity and emotional depth requires mindfulness—the willingness to be vulnerable and present with every emotion that surfaces.

11.6. Mindful Listening

The practice of singing is as much about listening as it is about vocalizing. Mindful listening requires an open and non-judgmental stance. It's about fully engaging with the sounds surrounding you—other instruments, the acoustics of your environment, even the silence that forms the backdrop to your voice.

Real improvement often comes, not from the endless repetition of exercises, but from attentive listening and immediate adjustment. Mindful listening fosters this skill and magnifies its impact, allowing the singer to optimize their practice in real-time and respond more thoughtfully to the musical dialogue within a performance.

11.7. Evolving Mindfulness

While starting a journey, it is imperative to realize that mindfulness isn't a one-time achievement but a continuous process of growth. As you embed mindfulness into your practice, remember to be patient with yourself. Like any skill, it will take time to develop, and every singer's mindfulness journey will look different.

Stay open, and keep exploring the depths of your experience without judgment or an agenda. Foster a sense of curiosity towards your voice, your body, and the music, allowing space for unexpected insight or development. Remember, this is about more than just nailing a pitch or a rhythm—it's about building a long-term, fulfilling relationship with your voice.

In conclusion, the integration of mindfulness into singing requires continuous effort and patience. However, its benefits—enhanced concentration, emotional depth, a more attuned sense of listening, and heightened self-awareness—are extensive and transformative. By cultivating mindfulness, you render a gift, not only to your singing practice but also to your broader journey of self-discovery.